DISCARD

WEST GEORGIA REGIONAL LIBRARY SYSTEM
Neva Lomason Memorial Library

America, My Country
Native Peoples

The Inuit

By Doraine Bennett

Content Review, With Special Thanks
Bernice M. Joseph, Ph.D. Candidate
Koyukon Athabascan
Vice Chancellor for Rural, Community and Native Education
University of Alaska Fairbanks
Fairbanks, Alaska

STATE STANDARDS PUBLISHING

Your State • Your Standards • Your Grade Level

Dear Educators, Librarians and Parents . . .

Thank you for choosing books from State Standards Publishing! This book supports state Departments of Educations' standards for elementary level social studies and has been measured by the ATOS Readability Formula for Books (Accelerated Reader), the Lexile Framework for Reading, and the Fountas & Pinnell Benchmark Assessment System for Guided Reading. Photographs and/or illustrations, captions, and other design elements have been included to provide supportive visual messaging to enhance text comprehension. Glossary and Word Index sections introduce key new words and help young readers develop skills in locating and combining information. "Think With Bagster" questions provide teachers and parents with tools for additional learning activities and critical thinking development. We wish you all success in using this book to meet your student or child's learning needs.

Jill Ward, President

Publisher
State Standards Publishing, LLC
1788 Quail Hollow
Hamilton, GA 31811, USA
1.866.740.3056, www.statestandardspublishing.com

Cataloging-in-Publication Data
Bennett, Doraine.
 The Inuit / Doraine Bennett.
  p. cm. -- (America, my country Native Peoples)
 Includes index.
 ISBN 978-1-935884-89-7 (lib. bdg.)
 ISBN 978-1-935884-95-8 (pbk.)
 1. Inuit Indians--Juvenile literature. 2. Eskimos--Juvenile literature. I. Title.
 970.004--dc23
                                           2012948403

Copyright © 2013 by State Standards Publishing, LLC. All rights reserved. No part of this book may be reproduced, stored, or transmitted in any form or by any means without prior written permission from the publisher. Printed in the United States of America, North Mankato, Minnesota, August 2012, 060512.

About the Author

Doraine Bennett has a degree in professional writing from Columbus State University in Columbus, Georgia, and has been writing and teaching writing for over twenty years. She is a published author of numerous books for children, as well as magazine articles for both children and adults. She is the editor of the National Infantry Association's *Infantry Bugler* magazine. Doraine enjoys reading and flower gardening. She lives in Georgia with her husband, Cliff.

1 2 3 4 5 – CG – 17 16 15 14 13

Table of Contents

How Do You Say Snow? 5

At Home in the Arctic 6

The Arctic Tundra 9

Using Resources 10

Hunting for Food 13

Staying Warm 14

Building a House 17

Getting Around 18

The Whale Hunt 21

Laughter Is Good Medicine 22

The First Outsiders 25

Conflict 26

The Inuit Today 29

Glossary 30

Index 31

Think With Bagster 32

Hi, I'm Bagster! Let's learn about Native Peoples.

How is life here similar to the way you live? How is it different?

4 The Inuit live in a land of ice and snow.

How Do You Say Snow?

The Inuit live in a land of ice and snow for nine to ten months out of the year. Many years ago, survival depended on understanding the subtle, or slight, changes in the land and the sea. In English, we describe cold weather **precipitation** as ice, sleet, slush, hail, and snow. The Inuit hunter had to know exactly what kind of snow and ice he might find as he tracked a caribou, a large deer sometimes called a reindeer. He needed to understand the precise, or exact, condition of the ice and snow. One Inuit language spoken in Alaska, called Inupiaq (in-you-pee-ack), has dozens of words and terms to describe these conditions.

Many **archaeologists** and other scientists believe the early Inuit people **migrated** from Asia. They may have come across a land bridge over the Bering Strait between Siberia and Alaska. Much of the land they crossed is now underwater, so the evidence that might show this crossing is hidden. Most scientists agree that the early Inuits had probably spread from present-day Alaska into Canada and Greenland between 900 and 1050 A.D.

The Inuit and other native peoples have their own beliefs about how they came to be. These beliefs are often different from what scientists think. In one Inuit creation story, a spirit being called Raven created human beings and all living things, including the sun and the moon.

At Home in the Arctic

The Inuit lived in the Arctic, one of the coldest, most severe places on earth. They were scattered across thousands of miles of land. Today they continue to live in four different countries. Find the United States, Canada, Russia, and Greenland on the map. Inuits in the United States live on islands of the Bering Sea and in Alaska. Groups of Canadian Inuit live in Nunavut, the Northwest Territories, Yukon, Labrador, and Quebec. The Siberian Inuit live on the northeast coast of Russia where the northern Pacific Ocean joins the Arctic Ocean. The Greenland Inuit live on the east and the west coasts of southern Greenland where the northern Atlantic Ocean joins the Arctic Ocean.

The Inuit sometimes see the northern lights, also called the **aurora borealis**. They appear as a greenish glow in the Arctic night sky. They stretch like ribbons across the horizon. The strange light is caused by solar particles from the sun striking magnetic atoms in the earth's atmosphere.

Map work:
- Can you find the Arctic Circle?
- The northern Pacific Ocean joins the Arctic Ocean at what seas?
- The northern Atlantic Ocean joins the Arctic Ocean at what seas?
- Which group of Inuit lives near the Hudson Bay?

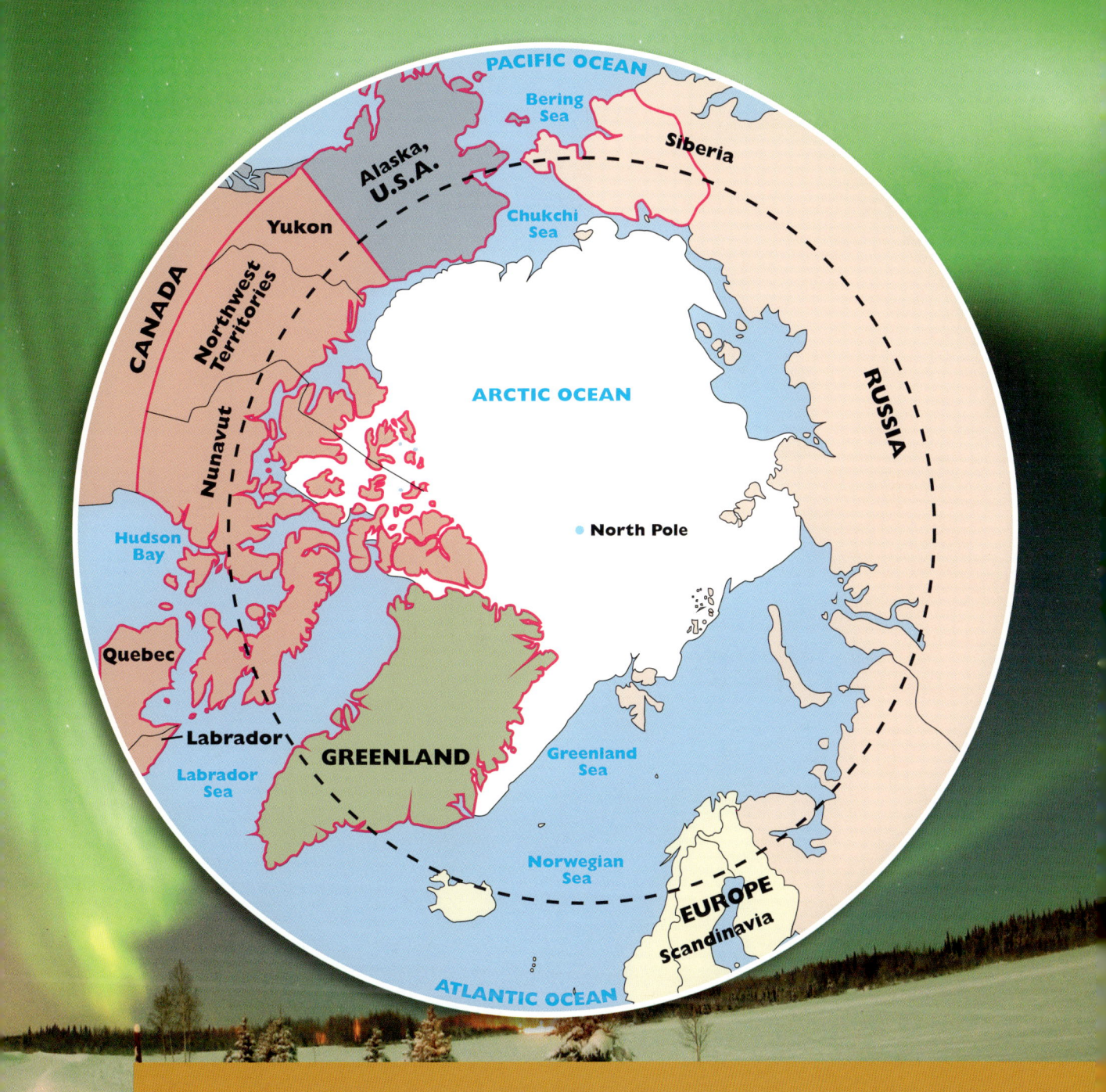

The Inuit are scattered across thousands of miles of land in the Arctic.

7

8   The Arctic tundra, where the Inuit live, is a treeless, cold plain.

The Arctic Tundra

The Arctic, where the Inuit live, is a treeless, cold plain often called the **tundra**. The soil beneath the ground is frozen solid, so most plants cannot grow. Their roots cannot pierce the icy ground, called **permafrost**. The land is covered with snow most of the year. The temperature can drop as low as 40 degrees below zero (–40°F) in winter. And from October to February, the sun does not rise at all.

Summers are short, usually from mid-July to late August. Milder temperatures cause the ice to melt, creating bogs and ponds. Many plants with shallow root systems can grow in the cold, such as grasses, moss, lichens, and low shrubs. The weather, the seasons, and the movement of animals in the tundra determined the lifestyle of the Inuit people.

Some people call this area the Land of the Midnight Sun. For a period of time during the summer, the sun does not set.

Using Resources

Survival in the Arctic was difficult. The Inuit had to depend on one another. If children became orphaned, without parents, other families adopted them. No one could survive alone.

The Inuit used everything available to them. They built homes from ice and snow and from driftwood brought in by the tides. Melted snow became drinking water. Clothes were made from animal skins and fur. Wildlife provided food. The men fished and hunted in one-man boats called **kayaks** made from driftwood and seal skins. Stone figures called **inuksuk** (in-ook-sook) helped guide the way or communicate messages to Inuit hunters and travelers. When a whale was killed, no part of it was wasted. The Inuit people ate the meat. They melted the **blubber** for oil and used it to cook, keep warm, and light their houses. They fashioned tools from whale bones and teeth. They even used whale whiskers to make snares for catching birds.

Whales, and other things from nature, are **natural resources**. **Human resources** are the people who produce goods or services from natural resources. An Inuit woman used a whalebone knife, called an **ulu** (oo-loo), to skin the animals. The ulu was a **capital resource**, a good or service made from a natural resource. The Inuit woman used one capital resource, the ulu, to make another capital resource, clothing. The Inuit man might trade the skins for caribou meat. Trading was another way to use capital resources.

Inuksuk helped hunters and travelers find the way.

What kinds of resources are being used in this picture?

The Inuit depended on all the resources available to them.

11

12   Trained dogs helped the Inuit hunt polar bears.

Hunting for Food

Since few plants grew in the frozen Arctic ground, the Inuit ate mostly meat. They ate seal, whale, and walrus. They ate fish, birds, and land **mammals**, like caribou and polar bear. Mammals are animals with backbones that feed their young with milk. Sometimes the women found cranberries, blueberries, and the roots of willow trees to add to a meal. One whale could feed a community for an entire winter.

Inuits usually ate the meat raw. The toughest parts were sometimes boiled. The Inuit learned that eating only cooked meat could cause sickness. Scientists today have discovered that the raw meat had vitamins and minerals in it that kept the Inuit from getting diseases like scurvy. Scurvy is a terrible disease caused by not eating foods with vitamin C, like vegetables and fruits. Cooking the meat would destroy or damage these vitamins and minerals.

In summer, herds of caribou migrated north. Inuit hunters often hid in a pit until the animal came near. Trained dogs helped them hunt polar bears, but this was dangerous. A hunter had to be very close to the bear to throw the spear. To keep the meat fresh, the men dug a pit and lined it with rocks. The meat stayed frozen until it was ready to be eaten.

Staying Warm

Warm, dry clothes could mean the difference between life and death in such a cold climate. Clothes were made from animal skins and fur. Waterproof boots made of seal skin were best for hunting on ice. Boots from caribou skin were warmer for hunting on land. Long pants and a **parka** were made of two layers of skins with the fur side against the body for warmth. The parka was a large, thick coat with a hood. The hood on a woman's parka was large enough for the baby on her back to stay warm. Parkas were snug at the wrists, neck, and waist to keep cold air out. Mittens that came up to the elbows kept their hands warm.

The Inuit made goggles of wood, ivory, or bone to protect their eyes. Sunlight reflecting on the snow could be so bright it harmed the eyes. The goggles reduced the sunlight and helped prevent blindness. Some Inuit wore earrings or nose rings as decorations. Women often wore tattoos on their faces to show they were ready to marry, and to keep evil spirits away.

Modern Inuit wear shirts and jeans much like you do when indoors. But staying warm outside is still a challenge. Many people still wear traditional parkas and boots, handmade by the women using animal skins and fur. But store-bought parkas and boots are available, too. Some still wear goggles to protect the eyes.

Warm, dry clothes could mean the difference between life and death in the cold climate.

15

16   The Inuit built igloos of snow and ice blocks when they were traveling.

Building a House

Most people think all Inuit houses in the Arctic were **igloos**. But that's not true. The Inuit built igloos of snow and ice blocks when they were traveling. These houses were very warm and could be built in about an hour. In summer, when the people followed the seal runs or caribou trails, they built tents from sticks and skins that could be moved easily.

Permanent houses for the winter months were dug into the ground, lined with sticks, and then covered with patches of grass and soil called sod. The entrance to both the igloo and the sod house was a long, underground tunnel that blocked the cold air. A window opening could be covered with animal intestines. These thin membranes let light in but kept the cold out. A hole cut into the roof provided fresh air and allowed smoke to escape.

Permanent houses for the winter months were dug into the ground.

Getting Around

The Inuit built their kayaks to be used in the ocean. The kayak could be steered so quietly a hunter could sneak up on a seal or walrus. An Inuit man built his kayak to fit his body, so he would always prefer his own boat. Using another hunter's kayak could be very difficult. The hunter wore a special watertight parka that fastened around the hole in the kayak. The hunter could roll the kayak over and come up again without any water getting into his boat or clothes.

The Inuit built a larger boat, called an **umiak** (oo-mee-ack), to carry people and supplies. It was often paddled by women. Kayaks and umiaks were made of driftwood or whale bones with animal skins stretched over the frame.

For travel on land, the Inuits made sleds by tying a platform onto wooden or whalebone runners. The runners worked like a pair of skis. A team of dogs, called huskies, pulled the sled.

What's in a Name?
The Inuit people have been called Eskimos. The name was used by early Europeans and came from the Native American word meaning "eater of raw meat." Some Inuit consider this term an insult. They call themselves Inuit, which means "the people." Some Inuit in Alaska and Russia prefer to be called Yup'ik.

The kayak was a one-man boat built for the ocean.

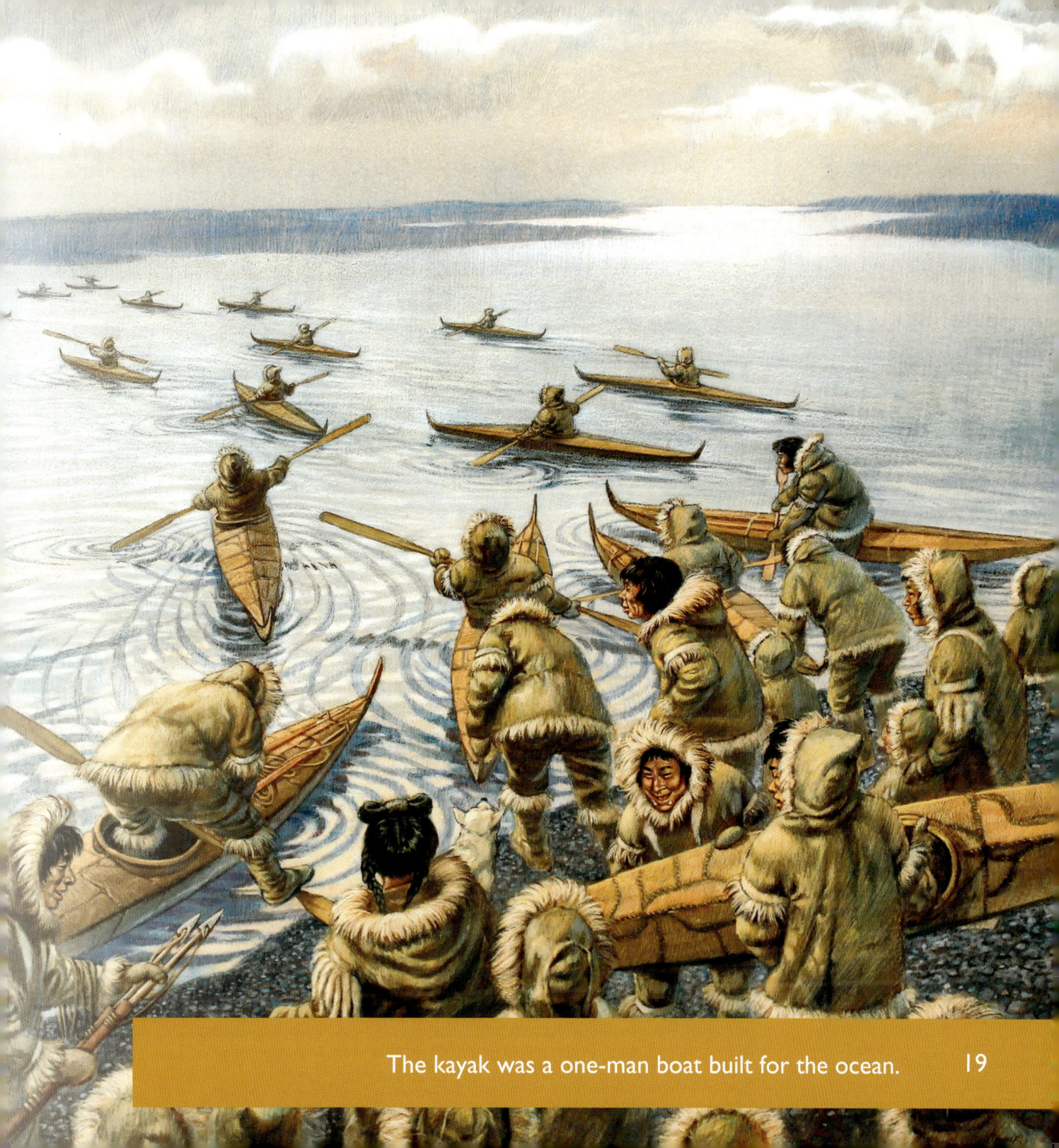

Hunters sang songs while dragging the whale home.

The hunters paddled as close to the whale as possible.

The Whale Hunt

The Inuit believed animals had souls that became monsters if the animal was mistreated. Even today, hunters are careful to respect the animal and be thankful to the whale for letting them kill and eat it.

Whale hunting is dangerous. The hunt began with dances, drumming, and songs. Hunters wore new, clean clothes as a sign of respect for the whale. The hunters paddled out to sea in umiaks. Others followed in kayaks. Each umiak carried a crew of at least four men—a steersman, a harpooner, and crew members. The hunters paddled as close to the animal as possible, then the harpooner threw his weapon into the whale's body. Small buckets and sealskin floats attached to the **harpoon** tired the whale as it tried to swim away. Other hunters joined the chase. Eventually they killed the exhausted whale with another type of spear called a lance.

While the men hunted whales, the women worked at home on their traditional tasks. They wove baskets, made parkas and boots, and searched for birds' eggs, seaweed, and edible plants, roots, and berries. They visited with one another and laughed together at shared stories.

While dragging the whale home, the hunters sang songs like this one:
You that we are towing along, Ah, ya ah e ya
Big whale, big whale, stir up the sea with your tail, E ya ah e ya
Give us fair weather today so we arrive safe and sound on shore, E ya ah e ya
Tug-tug along hard, E ya ah e ya, Row-row

Laughter Is Good Medicine

The Inuit moved around a lot. Hunting and fishing trips could keep families apart for many months. When they were together, they enjoyed feasts that included games, storytelling, and laughter. Humor was an important part of survival in the far north and is today. Have you ever tried to watch someone laugh? Did you begin laughing, too? That's exactly what happens in an Inuit laughing game. Two players face each other and hold hands. At a signal, they start to laugh. The person who laughs the longest and hardest is the winner. Everyone watching starts laughing, too. Sometimes people laugh so hard they roll on the floor.

Another Inuit tradition is throat singing. Two singers, usually women, face each other and **synchronize** their movements. They use their abdominal muscles to inhale and exhale short, sharp breaths. The leader produces a sound in the throat and the other singer responds. The first one to run out of breath or start laughing loses the game.

Today's Inuit still play games that develop strength, endurance, and mental focus. Some athletes compete in an "Arctic Winter Games" event. These games and sports may look like play, but they are really training for survival in the Arctic.

What kinds of stories do you think this person might be telling?

The Inuit enjoyed feasts that included games, storytelling, and laughter.

23

Vikings from Scandinavia encountered the Inuit in Greenland.

24 The Inuit had little contact with Europeans until the 1800s.

The First Outsiders

Because the Inuit lived in such faraway lands, they had little contact with Europeans. Scientists believe that Vikings from Scandinavia may have encountered the Inuit in Greenland around the year 1000. Almost six hundred years later, an English explorer named Martin Frobisher encountered the Inuit in Canada. He came looking for a northwest passage from Europe to China and India. In 1741, Vitus Bering's expedition from Russia met the Inuit of today's Alaska.

In the 1800s, fur traders, explorers, and fishermen came. Missionaries, a type of priest, arrived to teach the Inuit about the Christian religion. The Inuit usually had good relationships with some of these foreign people and taught them how to survive in the cold climate. But there was sometimes conflict, too.

Conflict

In the 1800s, Canadian and American whaling ships began sailing into Arctic waters. The sailors often lived on Inuit land during the winter months. The Inuit people gave them oil, blubber, and furs to stay warm. In return, the visitors offered tea and tobacco, flour and molasses, and guns and ammunition. Unfortunately, the sailors also brought diseases to the Inuit people. Smallpox, influenza, measles, and scarlet fever killed many of the Inuit.

In the 1900s, gold and oil were discovered in Inuit lands. As more people came, more conflict erupted. Later during World War II, airfields, weather stations, and radar lines were constructed on Inuit land. These land disputes in Alaska and Canada have taken years to resolve. In Alaska, Inuit groups finally gained legal ownership of their land in 1971. The government paid them for land used to develop the Alaska Pipeline that transports oil through the state. In Canada, a new territory called Nunavut was established on Inuit land in 1999. The Inuit in Canada govern this territory themselves.

The Inuit govern Nunavut in Canada.

The Alaska Pipeline runs across a portion of Inuit land in Alaska.

Modern Homes and City

Whale Hunting

Tourist Guide

"The sea ice is our highway."

Inuit Circumpolar Council – Canada

Do you think the Inuit might be concerned about climate change? Why or why not? Explain your own concerns.

28

The Inuit Today

In many places, the Inuit have moved to live in cities, but they have preserved their culture in spite of the interaction with non-native people. Their communities continue to speak Inupiaq and other Inuit languages. Students learn to make traditional clothes, mittens, and boots. They learn how to construct a sled, and skin and dress a freshly killed caribou. Hunting traditional foods is still an important part of the Inuit diet and way of life. Whaling is still an important Inuit industry.

Inuit carvings and paintings are popular in the art world and provide income for Inuit artists. Tourism is another source of income. Many communities have guides who take visitors sightseeing, big game hunting, or on dog team expeditions.

The Inuit face a new problem today—climate change. Hunters have noticed that the ice is thinner, the weather is more difficult to predict, and animals from farther south are found in their lands more often. The Inuit must learn to deal with these new problems using science and the knowledge and skills passed to them for generations.

The Inuit have formed a group called the Inuit Circumpolar Council. Its members come from Alaska, Canada, Greenland, and Russia. The Council provides a way to help the Inuit communicate and work together on issues that are important to all Inuit.

Glossary

archaeologists – Scientists who learn about past human life by studying objects left by ancient people.

aurora borealis – Glowing lights in the Arctic sky caused by solar particles from the sun striking magnetic atoms in the earth's atmosphere. Also called northern lights.

blubber – The fat under the skin of a whale or seal.

capital resources – Goods produced and used to make other goods and services.

harpoon – A spear used to hunt whales and large fish.

human resources – People working to produce goods and services.

igloo – A dome-shaped house made from blocks of ice or hard snow.

inuksuk – Stone figures built by the Inuit to help guide the way or communicate messages to other Inuit hunters and travelers.

kayak – A covered, narrow boat in which you sit and move through water by paddling.

mammals – Warm-blooded animals with backbones that feed their young with milk.

migrated – Moved from one country or region to another.

natural resources – Things that come directly from nature.

parka – A large, heavy jacket with a hood, usually made of fur or filled with down.

permafrost – Permanently frozen soil.

precipitation – The falling of water from the sky in the form of rain, sleet, hail, or snow.

synchronize – To arrange events or movements so that they happen at the same time or in the same order.

tundra – A cold area of land in northern Europe, Asia, and Arctic regions where there are no trees, and the soil under the surface of the ground is permanently frozen.

ulu – A knife used by Inuit women.

umiak – A type of boat used by the Inuit for carrying supplies and people.

Index

Alaska, 5, 6, 18, 25, 26, 29
animal, 9 10, 13, 14, 17, 18, 21, 29
archaeologist, 5
Arctic, 6, 9, 10, 13, 17, 22, 26
Asia, 5
aurora borealis, 6
Bering, 5, 6, 25
bird, 10, 13, 21
blubber, 10, 26
bone, 10, 13, 14, 18
boots, 14, 21, 29
Canada, 5, 6, 25, 26
caribou, 5, 10, 13, 14, 17, 29
climate, 14, 25, 29
clothes, 10, 14, 18, 21, 29
cold, 5, 6, 9, 14, 17, 25
conflict, 25, 26
disease, diseases, 13, 26
dogs, 13, 18, 29
driftwood, 10, 18
English, 5, 25
Europe, Europeans, 18, 25
explorers, 25
families, 10, 22
fish, fishermen, 10, 13, 22, 25
food, 10, 13
frozen, 9, 13

fur, 10, 14, 25, 26
game, 22, 29
grass, 9, 17
Greenland, 5, 6, 25, 29
harpoon, 21
home, house, 10, 17, 21
hunter, hunting, 5, 10, 13, 14, 18, 21, 22, 29
ice, 5, 9, 10, 14, 17, 29
igloos, 17
inuksuk, 10
Inupiaq, 5, 29
kayaks, 10, 18, 21
land, 5, 6, 9, 13, 14, 18, 25, 26, 29
mammals, 13
man, men, 10, 13, 18, 21
meat, 10, 13, 18
migrated, 5, 13
moved, movement, 9, 17, 22, 29
Nunavut, 6, 26
ocean, 6, 18
parka, 14, 18, 21
permafrost, 9
plants, 9, 13, 21
precipitation, 5
religion, 25

resources, 10
Russia, 6, 18, 25, 29
sea, 5, 6, 21, 28
seal, 10, 13, 14, 17, 18, 21
Siberia, 5, 6
skin, 10, 14, 17, 18, 21, 29
sled, 18, 29
snow, 5, 9, 10, 14, 17
spirit, 5, 14
summer, 9, 13, 17
sun, sunlight, 5, 6, 9, 14
survival, survive, 5, 10, 25
synchronize, 22
trade, traders 10, 25
tradition, 14, 21, 22, 29
travel, traveling, 10, 17, 18
tundra, 9
ulu, 10
umiak, 18, 21
United States, 6
walrus, 13, 18
warm, 10, 14, 17, 26
weather, 5, 9, 21, 26, 29
whale, whaling, 10, 13, 18, 21, 26, 29
winter, 9, 13, 17, 22, 26
woman, women, 10, 13, 14, 18, 21, 22

Editorial and Image Credits

Designer: Michael Sellner, Corporate Graphics, North Mankato, Minnesota
Consultant/Marketing Design: Alison Hagler, Basset and Becker Advertising, Columbus, Georgia

Images © copyright contributor unless otherwise specified.
Cover – "Inuit Beluga Whale Hunt" by Lewis Parker/lewisparker.ca. **4/5** – Young Hunter: Clark James Mishler. **6/7** – Map: Cheryl Graham/iStockphoto; Aurora: Wikipedia PD – USAF Senior Airman Joshua Strang. **8/9** – Tundra: Dentren/Wikipedia CC-BY-SA-3.0; Midnight Sun: V Berger/Wikipedia. **10/11** – Family: "Inuit Family Inside an Igloo" by Gordon Miller; Inuksuk: AgitatePhoto/iStockphoto. **12/13** – Mary Evans Picture Library/Alamy. **14/15** – Clothing: NativeStock; Goggles: Picture Contact BV/Alamy. **16/17** – Igloos: North Wind Picture Archives; Interior – Universal Images Group/Alamy. **18/19** – Hunters: See cover; Man: ArcticPhoto.com. **20/21** – "Narwhal Whales" by Else Bostelman; Hunters: NativeStock. **22/23** – North Wind Picture Archives. **24/25** – "First Communication with the Natives" by John Murray after John Sackheouse. **26/27** – Pipeline: Roger Asbury/iStockphoto; Map: Wikipedia. **28/29** – City: Jeangagnon/Wikipedia; Whaler: Loetscher Chlaus/Alamy; Guide: H. Mark Weidman Photography/Alamy

Think With Bagster

Use the information from the book to answer the questions below.

1. The Inuit have many words to describe snow and ice. Can you think of other words you use to describe rain, snow, or ice in English?

2. Find a map of the Arctic that has a scale. Can you determine how many miles the Inuit in Greenland are from the Inuit in Siberia?

3. Pretend you are an Inuit boy or girl, a human resource. Choose one natural resource available to you in the Arctic and tell what capital resource you could make from it.

4. Try playing the Inuit laughing game and see what happens.

Special Project

Most scientists agree that earth's climate, or weather, has changed over the last several hundred years. Temperatures and sea levels have gone up slightly. Sea ice and glaciers have been reduced. However, scientists do not agree on what has caused the change. Some say it is a natural cycle—from warm to cold to warm again. They believe the earth moves through these cycles in response to the sun. Others say the warming is caused by human activities that produce a gas called carbon dioxide. This gas gets trapped in earth's atmosphere, causing the temperature to rise. Burning fossil fuels like gasoline is an example. Some scientists believe climate warming is very dangerous and that many species of animals or plants may become extinct as a result. They believe the government should make laws to force people to change the way they use fossil fuels. Others say the danger is not that great. The issue is a hot one. Do your own research and decide what you believe.